Three Little Kittens and other favorite NURSERY RHYMES

Selected and illustrated by

TONY ROSS

Henry Holt and Company ❧ New York

Henry Holt and Company, LLC
Publishers since 1866
175 Fifth Avenue
New York, New York 10010
www.HenryHoltKids.com

Library of Congress Control Number: 2008925587

ISBN-13: 978-0-8050-8885-4
ISBN-10: 0-8050-8885-7

First American Edition—2009
Printed in Singapore on acid-free paper. ∞

1   3   5   7   9   10   8   6   4   2

To Zöe, Kate, Alex, Pip, and Saff

CONTENTS

"Grandad," said Nelly, "tell me a story, not a made-up one. One about real things."

"I don't know any stories about real things," said Grandad, scratching his nose, "but I do have this book of nursery rhymes. Some of those are about real things, real things that happened many years ago. Mostly, though, they teach something."

"What are nursery rhymes?" asked Nelly, looking very serious.

"Well," said Grandad, "let's read them together and find out."

THREE LITTLE KITTENS

Three little kittens, they lost their mittens,
And they began to cry.
"Oh mother dear, we sadly fear,
That we have lost our mittens."
"What! Lost your mittens, you naughty kittens!
Then you shall have no pie."
"Meow, meow, meow, now we shall have no pie."

The three little kittens, they found their mittens,
And they began to cry.
"Oh mother dear, see here, see here,
For we have found our mittens."
"Put on your mittens, you silly kittens,
And you shall have some pie."
"*Meow, meow, meow,* now let us have some pie."

The three little kittens put on their mittens,
And soon ate up the pie.
"Oh mother dear, we greatly fear,
That we have soiled our mittens."
"What! Soiled your mittens, you naughty kittens!"
Then they began to cry.
"Meow, meow, meow." Then they began to sigh.

The three little kittens, they washed their mittens,
And hung them out to dry.
"Oh mother dear, do you not hear
That we have washed our mittens?"
"What! Washed your mittens, you are good kittens,
But I smell a rat close by."
"*Meow, meow, meow,* we smell a rat nearby."

PUSSY CAT, PUSSY CAT

Pussy cat, pussy cat, where have you been?

I've been up to London to look at the queen.

Pussy cat, pussy cat, what did you there?
I frightened a little mouse under her chair.

"MEOW!"

WHAT ARE LITTLE BOYS MADE OF?

What are little boys made of?
Snips and snails and puppy dogs' tails.
That's what little boys are made of!

WHAT ARE LITTLE GIRLS MADE OF?

What are little girls made of?
Sugar and spice and all things nice.
That's what little girls are made of!

I Had a
Little Hen

I had a little hen, the prettiest ever seen,
She washed up the dishes and kept the house clean.
She went to the mill to fetch us some flour,
And always got home in less than an hour.
She baked my bread, she brewed my ale,
She sat by the fire and told a fine tale.

THERE WAS A CROOKED MAN

There was a crooked man,
Who walked a crooked mile.
He found a crooked sixpence,
Upon a crooked stile.
He bought a crooked cat,
Which caught a crooked mouse.
And they all lived together
In a little crooked house.

TWO LITTLE DICKY BIRDS

Two little dicky birds sitting on a wall,
One named Peter, one named Paul.
Fly away, Peter. Fly away, Paul.
Come back, Peter! Come back, Paul!

24

RING AROUND THE ROSY

Ring around the rosy,
A pocket full of posies.
Ashes, ashes!
We all fall down.

THIS LITTLE PIGGY

This little piggy
went to market,

This little piggy
stayed at home.

This little piggy
had roast beef,

This little piggy
had none.

And this little piggy went,

"WEE wee wee,"
all the way home.

Sing a Song
of Sixpence

Sing a song of sixpence,
a pocket full of rye,
Four and twenty blackbirds
baked in a pie.

When the pie was opened,
the birds began to sing.
Oh wasn't that a dainty dish
to set before the king?

The king was in his counting house,
counting out his money.
The queen was in the parlor,
eating bread and honey.

The maid was in the garden,
hanging out the clothes.
When down came a blackbird
and pecked off her nose.

SEE-SAW, MARJORY DAW

See-saw, Marjory Daw,
Johnny shall have a new master.
He shall earn but a penny a day,
Because he can't work any faster.

JACK SPRAT

Jack Sprat could eat no fat,
His wife could eat no lean.
And so between the two of them
They licked the platter clean.

One, Two, Three, Four, Five

One, two, three, four, five,

Once I caught a fish alive.

Six, seven, eight, nine, ten,

Then I let it go again.

Why did you let it go?

Because it bit my finger so.

Which finger did it bite?

This little finger on the right.

LADYBUG, LADYBUG!

Ladybug, ladybug!

Fly away home.

Your house is on fire,

And your children are gone.

All except one,

And that's little Ann,

For she crept under

The frying pan.

POLLY
PUT THE
KETTLE ON

Polly put the kettle on,
Polly put the kettle on,
Polly put the kettle on,
We'll all have tea.

Sukey take it off again,
Sukey take it off again,
Sukey take it off again,
They've all gone away.

LITTLE JACK HORNER

Little Jack Horner sat in the corner,
Eating his Christmas pie.
He put in his thumb and pulled out a plum
And said, "What a good boy am I!"

MARY, MARY

Mary, Mary, quite contrary,
How does your garden grow?
With silver bells and cockleshells
And pretty maids all in a row.

OLD MOTHER HUBBARD

Old Mother Hubbard

Went to the cupboard

To get her poor doggy a bone.

When she got there,

The cupboard was bare,

So the poor doggy had none.

CRY, BABY BUNTING

Cry, Baby Bunting,
Daddy's gone a-hunting,
Gone to fetch a rabbit skin
To wrap the Baby Bunting in.
Cry, Baby Bunting.

LITTLE TOMMY TUCKER

Little Tommy Tucker sings for his supper.

What shall we give him? Brown bread and butter.

How shall he cut it without a knife?

How shall he marry without a wife?

DOCTOR FOSTER

Doctor Foster went to Gloucester

In a shower of rain.

He stepped in a puddle

Right up to his middle,

And never went there again.

WISE
OLD OWL

A wise old owl

lived in an oak.

The more he saw,

the less he spoke.

The less he spoke,

the more he heard.

Why can't we all be like that wise old bird?

MARY HAD A LITTLE LAMB

Mary had a little lamb,
Its fleece was white as snow,
And everywhere that Mary went,
The lamb was sure to go.

It followed her to school one day,
Which was against the rule.
It made the children laugh and play
To see a lamb at school.

And so the teacher turned it out,
But still it lingered near,
And waited patiently about
'Til Mary did appear.

"Why does the lamb love Mary so?"
The eager children cry.
"Why, Mary loves the lamb, you know,"
The teacher did reply.

LITTLE
MISS MUFFET

Little Miss Muffet sat on a tuffet,
Eating her curds and whey.

Along came a spider,
Who sat down beside her,
And frightened Miss Muffet away.

The Itsy-Bitsy Spider

The itsy-bitsy spider
Climbed up the waterspout.
Down came the rain,
And washed the spider out.
Out came the sun,
And dried up all the rain.
And the itsy-bitsy spider
Went up the spout again.

SIMPLE SIMON

Simple Simon met a pieman
going to the fair.
Said Simple Simon to the pieman,
"Let me taste your ware."

Said the pieman to Simple Simon,
"Show me first your penny."
Said Simple Simon to the pieman,
"Sir, I have not any!"

Simple Simon went a-fishing
for to catch a whale;
All the water he had got
was in his mother's pail.

54

Simple Simon went to look
if plums grew on a thistle;
He pricked his fingers very much,
which made poor Simon whistle.

He went for water in a sieve
but soon it all fell through;
And now poor Simple Simon
bids you all adieu.

JACK
AND JILL

Jack and Jill went up the hill
To fetch a pail of water.
Jack fell down and broke his crown,
And Jill came tumbling after.
Up Jack got and home did trot
As fast as he could caper.
He went to bed to mend his head
With vinegar and brown paper.

GEORGIE PORGIE

Georgie Porgie, pudding and pie,

Kissed the girls and made them cry.

When the boys came out to play,

Georgie Porgie ran away.

RIDE A COCKHORSE

Ride a cockhorse to Banbury Cross
To see a fine lady upon a white horse.
With rings on her fingers and bells on her toes,
She shall have music wherever she goes.

HUMPTY DUMPTY

Humpty Dumpty sat on a wall,
Humpty Dumpty had a great fall.
All the king's horses and all the king's men
Couldn't put Humpty together again.

As I Was Going to St. Ives

As I was going to St. Ives,
I met a man with seven wives.
Each wife had seven sacks,
And in each sack were seven cats.
Each cat had seven kits.
Kits, cats, sacks, wives,
How many were going to St. Ives?

BAA, BAA, BLACK SHEEP

Baa, baa, black sheep, have you any wool?
Yes sir, yes sir, three bags full.
One for the master, one for the dame,
And one for the little boy who lives down the lane.

DING, DONG, BELL

Ding, dong, bell,
Pussy's in the well.
Who put her in?
Little Johnny Flynn.
Who pulled her out?
Little Tommy Stout.
What a naughty boy was that,
To try to drown poor pussy cat,
Who never did him any harm,
But killed all the mice in the farmer's barn!

RAIN, RAIN, GO AWAY

Rain, rain, go away,
Come again another day.
Little Johnny wants to play.
Rain, rain, go to Spain,
Never show your face again.

FOR WANT OF A NAIL

For want of a nail
The shoe was lost,
For want of a shoe
The horse was lost,

For want of a horse
The rider was lost,
For want of a rider
The battle was lost,
For want of a battle
The kingdom was lost,
And all for the want of a nail.

Goosey, Goosey, Gander

Goosey, Goosey, Gander,
Where shall I wander?
Upstairs, downstairs,
In my lady's chamber.
There I met an old man
Who wouldn't say his prayers.
I took him by the left leg,
And threw him down the stairs.

THE MAN IN THE WILDERNESS

The man in the wilderness asked me,
"How many strawberries grow in the sea?"
I answered him as I thought good,
"As many as herrings grow in the wood."

TOM, THE PIPER'S SON

Tom, he was a piper's son,
He learned to play when he was young.
But all the tunes that he could play
Was "Over the hills and far away."

PAT-A-CAKE,
PAT-A-CAKE

Pat-a-cake, pat-a-cake, baker's man,
Bake me a cake as fast as you can.

Pat it and prick it and mark it with a B,
Then put it in the oven for baby and me.

One, Two, Buckle My Shoe

1,2,
buckle my shoe,

3,4,
shut the door,

5,6,

pick up sticks,

7,8,

lay them straight,

9,10,

a good fat hen.

LITTLE BOY BLUE

Little Boy Blue,

come blow your horn.

The sheep's in the meadow,

the cow's in the corn.

But where is the boy

who looks after the sheep?

He's under a haystack fast asleep.

Will you wake him?

No, not I.

For if I do, he's sure to cry.

LITTLE ROBIN REDBREAST

Little Robin Redbreast sat upon a tree,
Up went pussy, and down went he,
Down came pussy, and away Robin ran;
Says Little Robin Redbreast, "Catch me if you can."
Little Robin Redbreast jumped upon a wall,
Pussy jumped after him and almost got a fall.
Little Robin chirped and sang, and what did pussy say?
Pussy said "Meow!" and Robin jumped away.

There Was an Old Woman

There was an old woman who lived in a shoe.
She had so many children she didn't know what to do.

ROCK-A-BYE BABY

Rock-a-bye baby in the treetop,

When the wind blows, the cradle will rock.

When the bough breaks, the cradle will fall,

And down will come baby, cradle and all.

Peter Piper

Peter Piper picked a peck of pickled pepper.
A peck of pickled pepper Peter Piper picked.
If Peter Piper picked a peck of pickled pepper,
Where's the peck of pickled pepper
Peter Piper picked?

PETER, PETER, PUMPKIN EATER

Peter, Peter, pumpkin eater,
Had a wife and couldn't keep her.
He put her in a pumpkin shell,
And there he kept her very well.

85

HEY, DIDDLE, DIDDLE

Hey, diddle, diddle,
the cat and the fiddle.
The cow jumped
over the moon.
The little dog laughed
to see such fun.
And the dish ran away
with the spoon.

THREE BLIND MICE

Three blind mice,
three blind mice—
See how they run!
See how they run!

They all ran after
the farmer's wife,
Who cut off their tails
with a carving knife.
Did you ever see
such a thing in your life
As three blind mice?

WEE WILLIE WINKIE

Wee Willie Winkie runs through the town,

Upstairs and downstairs in his nightgown,

Tapping at the window

and crying through the lock,

"Are all the children in their beds,

it's past eight o'clock!"

Hey, Willie Winkie, are you coming in?

The cat is singing purring sounds

to the sleeping hen,

The dog's spread out on the floor

But here's a wakeful little boy

who will not fall asleep!

"*It's past eight o'clock now, Grandad,*" *whispered Nelly, taking his hand.* "*Do you think Wee Willie Winkie will tap at my window tonight?*"

"*I very much doubt it,*" *said Grandad.* "*He must be terribly old by now! Come on, Nell. Time for bed.*"

INDEX OF FIRST LINES